Vikings

Teaching Tips

White Level 10

This book focuses on developing reading independence, fluency, and comprehension.

Before Reading
- Ask readers what they think the book will be about based on the title. Have them support their answer.

Read the Book
- Encourage readers to read silently on their own.
- As readers encounter unfamiliar words, ask them to look for context clues to see if they can figure out what the words mean. Encourage them to locate boldfaced words in the glossary and ask questions to clarify the meaning of new vocabulary.
- Allow readers time to absorb the text and think about each chapter.
- Ask readers to write down any questions they have about the book's content.

After Reading
- Ask readers to summarize the book.
- Encourage them to point out anything they did not understand and ask questions.
- Ask readers to review the questions on page 23. Have them go back through the book to find answers. Have them write their answers on a separate sheet of paper.

© 2024 Booklife Publishing
This edition is published by arrangement with Booklife Publishing.

North American adaptations © 2024 Jump!
5357 Penn Avenue South
Minneapolis, MN 55419
www.jumplibrary.com

Decodables by Jump! are published by Jump! Library.
All rights reserved. No part of this book may be reproduced in any form without written permission from the publisher.

Library of Congress Cataloging-in-Publication Data is available at www.loc.gov or upon request from the publisher.

ISBN: 979-8-88996-936-5 (hardcover)
ISBN: 979-8-88996-937-2 (paperback)
ISBN: 979-8-88996-938-9 (ebook)

Photo Credits
Images are courtesy of Shutterstock.com. With thanks to Getty Images, Thinkstock Photo and iStockphoto. Cover – Danny Smythe. p5 – El Greco 1973. p6–7 – Roninnw, Dr. Victor Wong, Kalleeck. p8–9 – Anna Krivitskaya, Olga Tashlikovich. p10–11 – Always Wanderlust, Anna Kepa. p12–13 – Anna Krivitskaya, El Greco 1973. p14–15 – Olga Makukha, PRESSLAB. p16–17 – Khosro, wjarek. p18–19 – Viktor Osipenko. p20–21 – MMACASSIR, NataliAlba.

Table of Contents

Page 4   Who Were the Vikings?

Page 6   The Gods

Page 8   Family

Page 10   Homes

Page 12   Food

Page 14   Viking Fashion

Page 16   Health and Medicine

Page 18   Being a Kid

Page 20   School and Learning

Page 22   Index

Page 23   Questions

Page 24   Glossary

Who Were the Vikings?

The Vikings were a group of people who lived from around 800 CE to 1050 CE. That was almost 1,000 years ago! Vikings lived in part of Europe that we now call Scandinavia. Vikings were not called Vikings when they were alive. They were known as Norsemen.

Where Vikings lived

There are lots of stories about Vikings. Vikings were known for being great sailors and soldiers. They traveled Europe attacking other groups. When they were at home, Vikings were also excellent farmers and fishers.

The Gods

The Vikings had a lot of gods. Just like the ancient Greeks, Romans, and Egyptians, the Vikings had gods for all sorts of things. Thor was the god of thunder and strength. Warriors **worshipped** Thor to become stronger before battles. Loki was the god of **mischief**.

Thor

Loki

Stories about gods were passed down through poems called the Eddas. There were stories about how the universe was created, the battles the gods fought to keep it safe, and how it would end. There was even a story about Odin giving away one of his eyes.

Odin

Family

Vikings had very close families. Many **generations** of Vikings often lived together. Vikings might have lived with their brothers, sisters, parents, and grandparents. There could have been up to 20 people living in one home. Vikings also kept many pets, such as dogs, cats, falcons, and even bears!

Vikings did not have family last names. Instead, they would take their father's name and add the Norse word for son or daughter to the end. So, if you were a boy, and your dad's name was Erik, then your last name might be Erikson.

Homes

Viking homes were called longhouses. Longhouses were just one long room. Most Viking families broke the room up into three smaller areas. One of the areas was used for the family's farm animals. Another area was used as a workshop. This left one space for the family to use.

Longhouses had a fire in the center. This fire was used for cooking, light, and heat. Life in a longhouse would have been pretty smelly and very loud.

Food

Vikings ate a lot of stew. They tried to make their food last a long time. Turning everything into stew was one way to **preserve** food and keep it fresh longer.

Vikings ate lots of meat and fish. They did eat some vegetables, but the vegetables were often put in the stew with meat. Vikings kept adding to the same stew pot as they took from it, so you could end up eating meat that had been in there for weeks.

Viking Fashion

Vikings put a lot of effort into looking good for each other. Compared to other groups of people who lived at the same time, Vikings were very clean. They bathed once a week, which was quite often in those days.

Vikings even wore jewelry!

Vikings were even known to carry little grooming pouches. Inside, they carried tweezers, razors, and combs. Most Viking men wore trousers and tunics, which were like long shirts. Viking women wore dresses. However, very rich Vikings wore clothes made with silk, gold, and animal furs from faraway lands.

Health and Medicine

In Viking times, it was very important to be strong. They had some interesting ways of trying to keep themselves strong and healthy. First, if Vikings believed a baby was not going to be strong enough, it is thought that they would leave the baby outside on its own.

Once Vikings made it to adulthood, they still had some very weird ways of treating **illnesses**. When Vikings got sick, some people would try and **cure** them using a song or poem. This was thought to be a magical cure that would scare away bad spirits.

Being a Kid

Viking childhood was very short. Viking boys were considered to be men by 16 years old, and girls were thought of as women by just 12 years old. Viking children were treated just like adults. They were expected to help their family by working on the farm and making food.

Even though Viking children had many jobs to do, they did get to play sometimes. Viking children even had toys, such as wooden swords, bows, and toy ships. As well as being fun, these toys were also used to train children for becoming adults.

School and Learning

Vikings did not go to school. But there was still plenty for Viking children to learn. Viking children had to learn how to read and write. Instead of using letters, Vikings wrote in shapes and symbols called runes.

Runes

Since there was no school, there were also no teachers. This means Viking children were taught everything by their parents. Children learned how to do the same things their parents did, such as cooking, sewing, and farming. They were also taught poems, songs, and stories about history.

Index

farmers 5
food 12, 18
longhouses 10–11
Odin 7

pets 8
poems 7, 17, 21
runes 20
Scandinavia 4

How to Use an Index

An index helps us find information in a book. Each word has a set of page numbers. These page numbers are where you can find information about that word.

Example: balloons 5, 8–10, 19

Important word

Page numbers

This means page 8, page 10, and all the pages in between. Here, it means pages 8, 9, and 10.

Questions

1. What were the Vikings known as when they were alive?

2. Who is the Viking god of thunder?

3. What toys did Viking children have?

4. Using the Table of Contents, can you find which page you can read about Viking fashion?

5. Using the Index, can you find a page in the book about pets the Vikings kept?

6. Using the Glossary, can you define what preserve means?

Glossary

cure:
To make a sick person feel better.

generations:
Descendants from a shared ancestor.

illnesses:
Sicknesses.

mischief:
Playful behavior that can be annoying or cause harm to others.

preserve:
To treat food so it doesn't go bad.

worshipped:
Honored a god.